THE SIX Week ROAD TRIP

SPEED LIMIT 65

EZ WIND

SUSAN CLOUT

Order this book online at www.trafford.com
or email orders@trafford.com

Most Trafford titles are also available at major online book retailers.

Printed in the United States of America.

ISBN: 978-1-4269-9459-3

Library of Congress Control Number: 2011916137

Trafford rev. 09/22/2011

 www.trafford.com

North America & international
toll-free: 1 888 232 4444 (USA & Canada)
phone: 250 383 6864 ♦ fax: 812 355 4082

This book is dedicated to Linda. We built a lasting friendship on this trip. I will cherish it forever.

The trip began on a Friday
With a show that couldn't be beat
Bonnie Raitt was the star with her Chuckles
And a band they called Little Feat.

Then, we drove through the night
And we drove through the day
In fact, we drove
Twenty-five hours away.

Some rest stops were dirty
Some rest stops were clean
With hundreds of
Really flat miles between.

At four in the morning
We arrived at the house
Of Linda's cousin, named Fran
And Len was her spouse.

We ate some pig
We ate some cow
We also had syrup
And it was like Wow!

On Monday the time came
To get back on the road
So we filled up our bags
And packed up our load.

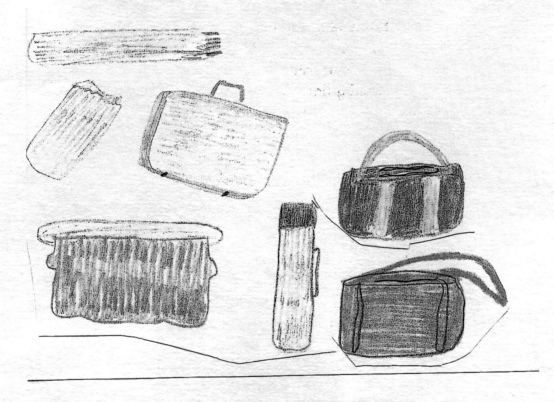

We drove through Ontario
For our very first time
We turned in our money
'cause they didn't take dimes.

When we got to New York
We came to a city
It was one known as Johnson
And Linda got giddy.

We finally arrived at
Long Island on Tuesday
We drank tea with Mike
And then read the Newsday.

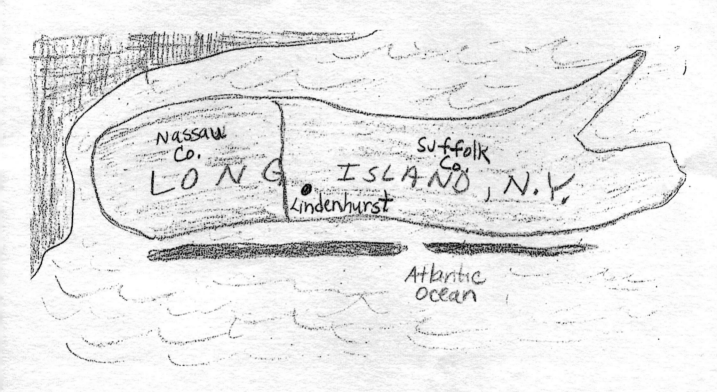

Again it was time
To go to a show
It was Dead all the way
From the 88th row.

The songs that they played
Were still in our heads
When at last the time came
To lay down in our beds.

On Wednesday we sailed
On the Great South Bay
We saw a nice sunset
At the end of the day.

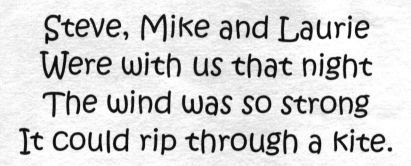

Steve, Mike and Laurie
Were with us that night
The wind was so strong
It could rip through a kite.

Manorville was on
The agenda for Thursday
We went on to Montauk
And there we did lay.

The sand was real hot
And the ocean was cold
But the time with the Jones'
Was better than gold.

On Friday we shopped
For food at the store
Then relaxed at Mike's house
Until it was four.

I made my burritos
And everyone ate
Until there was nothing
But stains on their plate.

The next day we celebrated
The fourth of July
We first stopped in Norwalk
For lunch and said hi!

We ate with Pete and Lynn
We ate with Bern and Art
We ate with other folks
Who I love with all my heart.

Then we cruised through Rhode Island
So Linda could buy
Yet another mug for coffee
Oh me, oh my!

By mid-afternoon
We headed for Boston
A really big city
we found ourselves lost in.

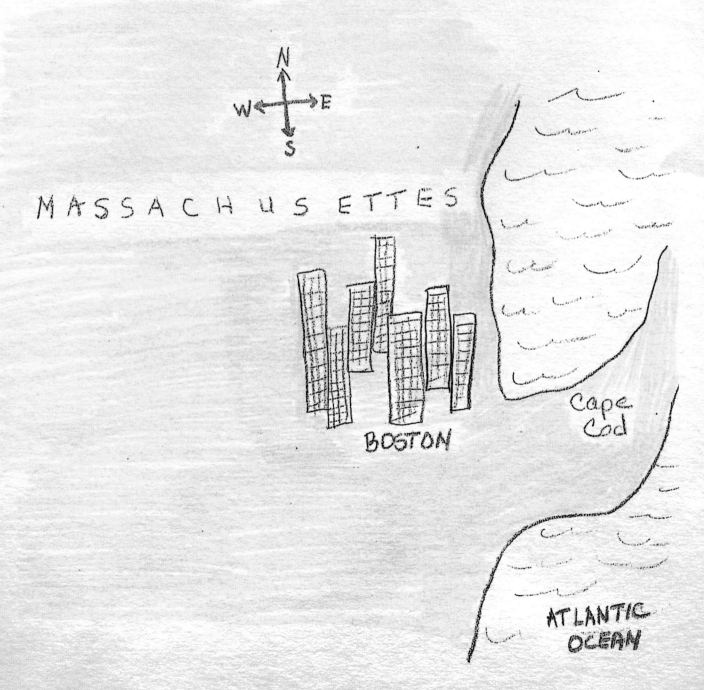

We ate dinner with Manny
And got ice cream cones too
Then we walked down the street
To see what was new.

What we saw was fantastic
It couldn't be beat
A fireworks display
That kept us out of our seats.

Now, Maine is the place
I wanted to go all along
Even Steve was inspired
And so wrote a song.

We got there on Sunday
Before it was noon
Mom wasn't there
But she'd arrive soon.

So we unpacked our bags
and emptied the truck
The mosquitoes were thick
Which was really bad luck.

But the lake was so pretty
And really inviting
I put on my suit
and ignored all the biting.

On Monday we ventured
To Bridgton to pick
Enough berries to make
A small army sick.

But Audrey's strawberry shortcake
Was quite a delight
It really was heaven
From the first to last bite.

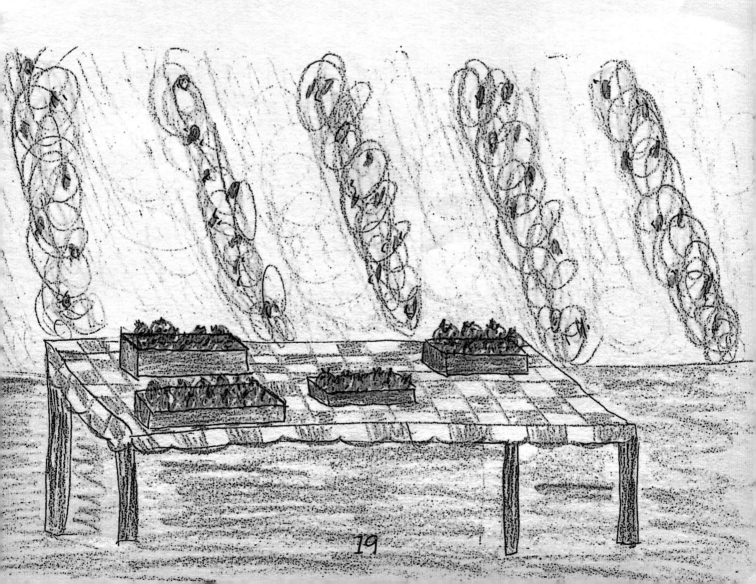

We did many fun things
When we were in Maine
It didn't matter the weather
We played in the rain.

One day we went hiking
Up old Bald Face
We quickly picked blueberries
Then kept up the pace.

At the end of the trail
Was a very cold pool
The time spent at Emerald
Was literally cool!

We went back to Long Island
For Diana's big day
She graduated high school
Then had a par-tay!

Linda spent her time
Recording a CD
Steve helped her a lot
Without charging a fee.

Diana went with us
as we headed back to the lake
we water skied and innertubed
in and out of the wake.

It was fun shopping
In North Conway, New Hampshire
And after a wonderful lunch
We spent time in the river.

We got set to leave
Without even a care
Then drove down the road
And saw a big bear!

Another day spent fishing
Another hiking Sabbattus
We even played golf
Although they would laugh at us.

One day I got
A most interesting call
I got a job
That would start in the fall.

For 35 years
I'd wanted to be a teacher
So lobster and gifts
Were that night's feature.

We finally left Maine
The third week in July
It was hard to leave home
But I did not cry.

Norwalk was on
The list for that night
We slept at aunt Bern's
After having a bite.

Then it was on to the Leeton's
We all went to a new show
It was Saving Private Ryan
Then to dinner we did go.

The next day was weird
When we found a big sword
The day in Sleepy Hollow
I was anything but bored.

Now Nancie and Warren
Sure like to have fun
They put tape on their faces
Acting sillier than my son.

On the road in the morning
I saw a sign
It said Beacon
Linda said that'd be fine.

I wanted to see
Where my mother was raised
It was 40 Ackerman St
I stood and I gazed.

We ate a good lunch
Near some falls in PA.
Then stayed with Aunt Lillie
At the end of the day.

The furniture that Linda
Wanted to go get
Was too old and worn out
She said she's all set.

It was back through Ontario
Another dinner at Fran's
A storm entering Denver
But really great tans.

Five thousand five hundred
Miles we traveled
And not even a stitch
Of our friendship unraveled.

No tickets, no accidents
No breakdowns we had
And on the 30th of July
We got back to our own pad.

Printed by
EDWARDS BROTHERS
www.edwardsbrothers.com
05SKC12MDJa